EXPLORERS

Francisco Vásquez de
Coronado

Kristin Petrie

ABDO
Publishing Company

visit us at
www.abdopublishing.com

Published by ABDO Publishing Company, 8000 West 78th Street, Edina, Minnesota 55439. Copyright © 2004 by Abdo Consulting Group, Inc. International copyrights reserved in all countries. No part of this book may be reproduced in any form without written permission from the publisher.

Printed in the United States of America, North Mankato, Minnesota.
012004 032011

Cover Photos: Corbis, North Wind
Interior Photos: Corbis pp. 5, 7, 8, 9, 10, 11, 13, 14, 19, 20, 24, 25, 29; North Wind pp. 15, 17, 21, 27

Series Coordinator: Stephanie Hedlund
Editors: Kate A. Conley, Kristin Van Cleaf
Art Direction & Cover Design: Neil Klinepier
Interior Design & Maps: Dave Bullen

Library of Congress Cataloging-in-Publication Data

Petrie, Kristin, 1970-
   Francisco Vásquez de Coronado / Kristin Petrie.
     p. cm. -- (Explorers)
   Summary: Traces the life and accomplishments of Spanish explorer and conquistador, Francisco Vásquez de Coronado, who led a major expedition from Mexico through what is now the southwestern United States.
   ISBN 1-59197-597-2
    1. Coronado, Francisco Vâsquez de, 1510-1554--Juvenile literature. 2. Explorers--America--Biography--Juvenile literature. 3. Explorers--Spain--Biography--Juvenile literature. 4. America--Discovery and exploration--Spanish--Juvenile literature. 5. Southwest, New--Discovery and exploration--Spanish--Juvenile literature. [1. Coronado, Francisco Vâsquez de, 1510-1554. 2. Explorers. 3. America--Discovery and exploration--Spanish. 4. Southwest, New--Discovery and exploration--Spanish.] I. Title.

E125.V3P48 2004
979'.01'092--dc22
[B]   2003062922

Contents

Francisco Vásquez de Coronado

In the 1500s, Spain was ready to take over the world. In particular, it was ready to take over the New World. Spaniards were leading the exploration of the newly discovered land.

In 1521, Spaniard Hernán Cortés conquered the mighty Aztec Empire. He claimed all of Mexico for Spain. However, the Spaniards sought more gold and riches like those found in the Aztec's empire. This drove them to unknown lands.

By 1540, much of the land from Hispaniola to Mexico was under Spanish rule. Now, it was time to expand to the north. One of the men to take this challenge was Francisco Vásquez de Coronado.

1451
Christopher Columbus born

1485
Hernán Cortés born

1450
John Cabot born

1460
Vasco da Gama born

1491
Jacques Cartier born

Coronado may have been the most determined of all the Spanish explorers. From 1540 to 1542, he led an elaborate mission in search of the New World's riches. Continue reading to discover what he found.

Coronado leading his army

1492
Columbus's first voyage west for Spain

1496
Cabot's first voyage for England

1493
Columbus's second voyage, attempted to colonize Hispaniola

Early Years

In 1510, Francisco Vásquez de Coronado was born in Salamanca, Spain. His parents were Juan Vásquez de Coronado and Isabel de Luján. Francisco was the couple's second son.

Little is known about Francisco's early life. However, it is known that his father was a nobleman. It is also known that the Coronados lived in a university town. So, Francisco may have attended the best schools.

However, Francisco was not the oldest of Juan and Isabel's sons. So, he would not inherit his father's wealth. Francisco had to make a choice. He could remain in Spain and live on a small portion of his family's money. Or, he could look for his own riches.

1497
Cabot's second voyage, discovered the Grand Banks; da Gama was first to sail around Africa to India

1496 or 1497
Hernando de Soto born

1498
Cabot's third voyage, may have died; Columbus's third voyage

Would You?

Would you look for your own riches? What do you think you would have become if you had lived in the 1500s?

Coronado was born in the university town of Salamanca, Spain.

1502
Columbus's fourth voyage; da Gama's second voyage

1506
Columbus died

1504
Cortés sailed to the West Indies

New Spain

Francisco's search for riches led him to the New World. By 1521, Spanish armies had conquered the Aztec Empire there. Following this, the Spanish had started colonizing the area, calling it New Spain.

King Charles I

Spain's king Charles I had appointed Antonio de Mendoza to govern New Spain. In 1535, Francisco accompanied Mendoza on his voyage to the new colony.

In New Spain, Francisco met a woman named Beatriz de Estrada. Beatriz was the daughter of New Spain's late **treasurer**. Her family was wealthy, and they were cousins to King Charles I. Francisco and Beatriz were soon married. They had five children, one son and four daughters.

1511
Cortés helped take over Cuba

1510
Francisco Vásquez de Coronado born

1514
De Soto went to the New World

Francisco became an important figure socially and politically. In addition to marrying a noblewoman, Francisco had shown he was a good leader. He became a commander in the military. He settled arguments between the natives and the Spaniards. Francisco also stopped a **rebellion** of miners.

In 1538, Francisco was appointed to the city council of Mexico City. He was also made governor of Nueva Galicia, a **province** in western New Spain. After only three years in New Spain, Francisco had it all. He was wealthy, respected, and a leader in the government. What was next for this Spaniard?

Mexico City in the 1800s

Cabeza de Vaca

Coronado's next adventure was inspired by Pánfilo de Narváez. In 1528, Charles I had ordered Narváez on an expedition. It included an army of 300 soldiers. They were supposed to colonize the New World from La Florida to the west for Spain.

The expedition left Cuba for La Florida in 1528. After many problems, only four soldiers had survived. Álvar Núñez Cabeza de Vaca and three others had wandered through present-day Texas and northern Mexico.

In 1536, the four men entered Mexico City. Cabeza de Vaca met with Mendoza. He told of the survivors' eight long years of hardships. He also mentioned the stories he

Narváez and his men wait to be rescued.

1524
Da Gama's third voyage, died in Cochin, India

1519–1521
Cortés conquered the Aztec Empire and claimed Mexico for Spain

1532
De Soto helped attack the Inca Empire

Cabeza de Vaca and three others crossed the desert to enter Mexico City.

had heard from the natives. The stories told of wealthy nations north of the deserts and mountains.

Mendoza was very interested in the accounts of these wealthy nations. Many Spaniards believed a legend that said wealthy cities were to be found in the New World. Mendoza wondered, could these possibly be the Seven Cities of Cíbola?

THE SEVEN CITIES
● ● ●

In the 700s, North African warriors known as Moors conquered Spain. According to legend, around the year 714 seven bishops and their followers escaped Moorish rule in Spain. They built boats and crossed the Atlantic Ocean.

When they arrived at a new land, they built seven wonderful cities, called the Seven Cities of Cíbola. The bishops and their people filled them with gold and other riches.

By 1500, the Moors had been forced out of Spain. However, the legend remained. Many Spaniards believed the cities were to be discovered in the New World.

After Cabeza de Vaca's report, Mendoza quickly sent a group to scout the regions north of New Spain. If they found traces of the wealthy cities, a full expedition would be arranged. Marcos de Niza, a **Franciscan**, led the small group.

Niza returned five months later to report his findings to Mendoza. Niza claimed to have seen the outline of a huge city, larger than any in New Spain. He said the houses were ten stories high and their doors were decorated with **turquoise**.

The natives of the region were very hostile. So, Niza had turned back. But, he claimed to have seen more of the seven wealthy cities on the return journey.

1534
Cartier's first voyage for France

1539–1542
De Soto explored La Florida

1533
De Soto helped take over Cuzco

1535
Cartier's second voyage

Niza's large golden cities were actually adobe pueblos.

Conquistador

Mendoza was excited to take over these cities. On January 6, 1540, he appointed his friend, Coronado, to lead a full expedition. Coronado and an army would conquer the cities and claim them for Spain.

With this appointment, Coronado took on the role of conquistador. Conquistadors were Spanish explorers that were also military leaders. They used force to claim new territory and the land's resources. Often, they captured the area's natives and made them slaves.

Conquistadors, such as Coronado, often took the natives as slaves.

In April 1540, Coronado headed north from Compostela, the capital of Nueva Galicia. His army included 1,000 men and 1,500 horses and mules. Two ships were sent up the coast of present-day California to support the troops.

The group was an impressive sight. Coronado sat high on his horse. He wore a shiny golden **breastplate**, and a red feather on his helmet. The troops marched off into the desert with much **fanfare**.

Coronado wore golden armor with red accents, such as this.

1547
Cortés died

1557
Cartier died

1542
Coronado returned to New Spain; de Soto died

1554
Coronado died

1566
Drake's first voyage to the New World

The Seven Cities

In July, Coronado's army finally reached its **destination**, an area called Cíbola. It had been a long, hard journey through rough **terrain** and desert. Food had run low and there was little water. Many soldiers and animals had died along the way.

Háwikuh, the first of the fabled cities, was not the **oasis** they had hoped for. This first "golden city" was merely a village amid the rugged landscape. There were no guards in golden armor or jewels on the doors. Háwikuh was a pueblo, a village of **adobe** huts.

Members of the Zuni tribe lived in Háwikuh. The Zuni attempted to protect their villages. But, they were soon overtaken by the large army and its guns and **ammunition**. The same thing happened at each village the Spaniards encountered. Coronado claimed all of Cíbola for Spain.

1567
Drake's second voyage

1577
Drake began a worldwide voyage, was first Englishman to sail the Pacific Ocean

1570 and 1572
Drake terrorized the Spanish in the New World

Would You?

Would you be disappointed in Háwikuh? Do you think you would continue searching for the legendary cities?

Coronado may have used the Zuni-Acoma Trail on his search for Cíbola.

Continuing On

There was no gold in Cíbola. But were there cities of gold just over the next mountain? Were they around the next bend? Coronado did not give up.

The Zuni were eager to get rid of the soldiers. They encouraged Coronado to continue searching. They said the riches the Spaniards sought could be found in the northeast.

Coronado had been injured when his army overtook Háwikuh. He needed to heal and allow his army to rest. So, he sent three small groups to scout the regions to the north, west, and east of Cíbola.

Lieutenant García López de Cárdenas and his group traveled to the northwest. Not long into their search, the land dropped off in front of them. They became the first Europeans to see the Grand Canyon. Far below them snaked the Colorado River.

1588
Drake helped England win the Battle of Gravelines against Spain's Invincible Armada

1581
Drake knighted by Queen Elizabeth I

1596
Drake died

The Colorado River runs through the Grand Canyon.

1728
James Cook born

1765
Boone journeyed to Florida

1768
Cook sailed for Tahiti

1734
Daniel Boone born

1767
Boone explored Kentucky

**Coronado claimed the land
he explored for Spain.**

The second group, led by Captain Pedro de Tovar, was sent northeast. Its assignment was to search for a region called Tusayan. Tusayan was also said to have seven cities. They could possibly be the seven cities of gold. Tovar managed to find Tusayan, but it was another pueblo.

The third group explored to the east. Led by Hernando de Alvarado, this group found themselves in the Rio Grande Valley. Alvarado encouraged Coronado to bring his army to this rich land. There was no gold there, but food and other necessities were plentiful. Coronado moved his army to this region, called Tiguex, in the fall of 1540.

During their stay, the soldiers treated the natives of Tiguex poorly. They stole food and clothing. Natives were even forced out of their homes. The soldiers wanted to spend the cold winter in the warm huts.

The Spaniards' poor behavior led to tension and fighting. Soldiers stormed villages and killed many innocent native people. Soon, there was fear and hatred of the white men throughout the Rio Grande Valley.

Coronado's men camped along the Rio Grande.

1778
Cook became the first European to record Hawaiian Islands; Boone captured by Shawnee

1775
Boone cut the Wilderness Road from Virginia to Kentucky

1779
Cook died

Wyoming

Nebraska

Nevada

Utah

Colorado River

Colorado

G R E A T

Quivira

Kansas

California

Tusayan

*Grand
Canyon*

Cíbola Tiguex

Arizona Háwikuh

Oklahoma

P L A I N S

New
Mexico

*Palo Duro
Canyon*

Red River

Rio Grande

Pecos River

Texas

Rio Grande

**NEW SPAIN
(Mexico)**

Nueva Galicia

*Pacific
Ocean*

Compostela

Mexico City

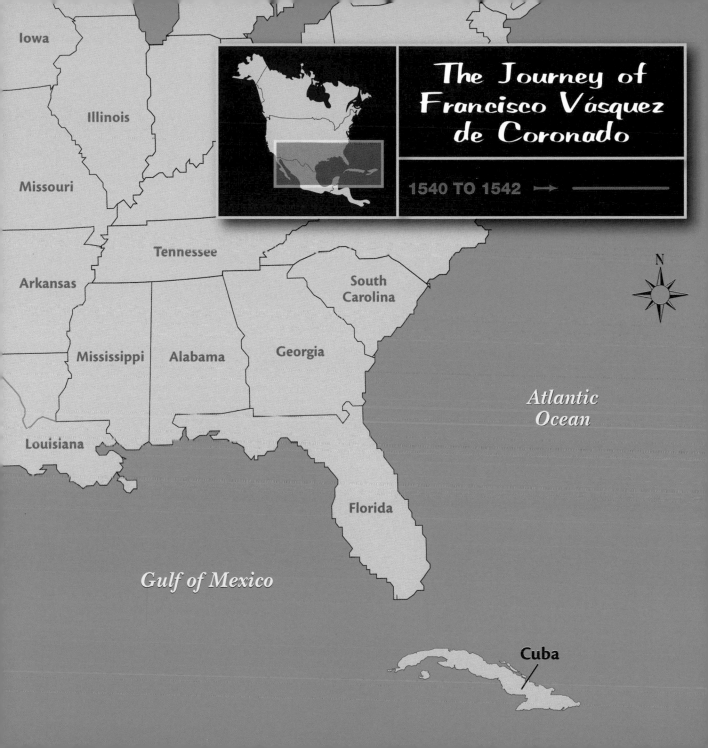

Iowa

Illinois

Missouri

Tennessee

Arkansas

South
Carolina

Mississippi   Alabama   Georgia

Louisiana

Atlantic
Ocean

Florida

Gulf of Mexico

Cuba

N

The Journey of
Francisco Vásquez
de Coronado

1540 TO 1542 ➤

Quivira

During the winter months, Coronado heard another story about a wealthy city to the northeast. It was called Quivira. Coronado led a search for its riches in the spring of 1541.

The army crossed the Pecos River. Then, the soldiers made their way through present-day Texas and Oklahoma. They were the first Europeans to see the millions of buffalo that roamed the **Great Plains**.

Midway into this journey, the army ran out of food. Coronado sent his troops back to the Rio Grande. But, he and 30 horsemen continued their search. Two native guides led Coronado's group.

Spaniards had never seen buffalo until Coronado explored the Great Plains.

1813
John C. Frémont born

1842
Frémont's first independent surveying mission

1820
Boone died

Would You?

Would you want to settle this new land? Do you think Coronado should have stayed?

On his search for Quivira, Coronado had two native guides. They said they knew where to find gold. However, their goal was to lead the Spaniards away from their people.

When Coronado and his group reached Palo Duro Canyon, they turned north. Soon the expedition crossed the plains of what is now Oklahoma. They finally reached the future state of Kansas, and what they believed was Quivira.

This city of gold was yet another group of native villages. The natives ran from the Spaniards' horses. They were frightened of these animals they had never seen before. Eventually, the natives gave the Spaniards food, pottery, and **turquoise**, but no gold.

The search for material riches turned up empty. Coronado did, however, find a region full of natural riches. The soil was black and moist. Trees and plants provided fruits, nuts, and other good crops. But, the weather was too cold, there were few people, and no gold. So, Coronado turned back.

1856
Frémont ran for president of the United States but lost

1845-1846
Frémont explored the Great Basin and the Pacific Coast, fought in the Mexican War

1890
Frémont died

Before Spaniards arrived, horses were not found in the New World. These animals frightened the native people and often caused them to flee in fear.

1910
Jacques Cousteau born

1951
Cousteau's first expedition in the Red Sea

1942
Cousteau and Gagnan developed the Aqua-Lung for diving

Final Days

A second attempt to find gold had failed. Coronado and his soldiers gave up their search. The group crossed back over the plains of Kansas, and spent their second winter in Tiguex.

Finally, in the spring of 1542, the group turned south to New Spain. More than two years after his grand departure, Coronado re-entered Mexico City.

Only about 100 men from Coronado's army returned from the mission. Most had died from injury or disease, or had **deserted** the expedition. Likewise, many native people had lost their lives as Coronado's army moved through their lands.

Coronado remained governor of Nueva Galicia. But then in 1544 his expedition was investigated, and he lost this position. He was charged with mistreatment of the natives and failure to settle the lands he had explored. Coronado was cleared of any wrongdoing in 1546. But, he never regained his title.

1997
Cousteau died

1974
Cousteau formed the Cousteau Society to protect marine life

The ruins of pueblos visited by Coronado can be found in Coronado State Monument in New Mexico.

Francisco Vásquez de Coronado died on September 22, 1554. He was buried in Mexico City. Coronado contributed much to the New World. He uncovered wonders such as the Grand Canyon and herds of wild buffalo. He also brought Spanish **culture** to the American Southwest.

Would You?

Would you consider Coronado's expedition a failure? Why or why not?

Glossary

adobe - a type of brick made from sun-dried earth and straw. It is used as a building material.

ammunition - bullets, shells, and other items used in firearms.

breastplate - a metal plate used as armor to protect the chest.

culture - the customs, arts, and tools of a nation or people at a certain time.

desert - to withdraw from or leave a group with no intention of returning.

destination - the place someone or something is going to.

fanfare - showy outward display.

Franciscan - a member of the Order of Friars Minor, who is dedicated to preaching, missions, and charities.

Great Plains - an area of grassy land between the Rocky Mountains and the Mississippi River.

oasis - a place in the desert with water, trees, and plants.

province - a geographical or governmental division of a country.

rebellion - an armed resistance or defiance of a government.

terrain - the physical features of an area of land. Mountains, rivers, and canyons can all be part of a terrain.

treasurer - a person who handles the money for a business, organization, or government.

turquoise - a gem that is bluish-green.

Saying It

Álvar Núñez Cabeza de Vaca - AHL-bahr NOON-yath
kah-BAY-thah thay BAH-kah
conquistador - kahn-KEES-tuh-dawr
Nueva Galicia - NWAY-vah gahleh-SYAW
Pánfilo de Narváez - PAHM-fee-loh thay nahr-BAH-ayth
Quivira - kih-VIHR-uh
Salamanca - sah-lah-MAHNG-kah
turquoise - TUHR-koyz

Web Sites

To learn more about Francisco Vásquez de Coronado, visit ABDO Publishing Company on the World Wide Web at **www.abdopublishing.com**. Web sites about Francisco Vásquez de Coronado are featured on our Book Links page. These links are routinely monitored and updated to provide the most current information available.

Jacques Cousteau *Sir Francis Drake* *Vasco da Gama*

Hernán Cortés *Hernando de Soto* *John C. Frémont*

Index